UNCULTURED Artist

One man
Few characters
Millions of Realities

AF530250

CHANDAN SHARMA

BlueRose ONE .com
Stories Matter
New Delhi • London

BLUEROSE PUBLISHERS
India | U.K.

ajay.parikh@hotmail.com

For permissions requests or inquiries regarding this publication, please contact:

BLUEROSE PUBLISHERS
www.BlueRoseONE.com
info@bluerosepublishers.com
+91 8882 898 898
+4407342408967

ISBN: 978-93-5989-308-2

Cover Design: Rishav Rai
Backcover Photo: Paayal Parikh
Typography Design: Rohit

First Edition: January 2024

ACKNOWLEDGEMENT

In producing 'Uncultured Artist,' I express my sincere gratitude to all of the numerous encounters that influenced my path. With particular thanks to my former partner, whose presence and influence have had a lasting impact on my artistic and character development; to my dance teacher, who taught me and supported me through my dance journey; to my family, who never left me even when I was on the wrong path; to my friends, who trusted me and supported me; and special thanks to one of my favorite people, Lisha, who helped me a lot in writing this book. I appreciate you participating in my artistic journey.

CONTENTS

1.

CHILDHOOD WAS A NIGHTMARE

"I never knew that humans could be judgmental at this level.'

My name is Manav, and I was born into a middle-class household. I was born a black boy. I was the only person of color in my family. So I was named Kaalu from birth because of my skin color. This was the most embarrassing moment for my parents, but they couldn't do anything because my family was full of old-fashioned people.

But then something miraculous happened to me. I began to turn white. But the identity they gave me lives on. I was raised by a struggling family. My father used to own a little shop, so it was a little difficult for him to manage, but he was able to meet our family's demands. My resources were really restricted at the time. As a result, I never received the same level of support as other youngsters. I rarely had in excess of a couple of toys. But every time I went outdoors and saw the other kids, I wished I could live their lives. Apart from me, I had one brother and four cousins. We were all around the same age. Even though we had six kids in total, I couldn't have that kind of fun because each time I tried to do something, someone yelled at me and occasionally hit me. I was just two years old at the time. My entire family consisted of my brother, my parents, four cousins, two uncles, two aunts, and my grandmother. However, there was no harmony between my father and his elder brother. As a result, he had less say in our family's decisions.

"Our mindset and actions create our aura, and our aura represents our true character'.

My older aunt was a weird woman who lacked ethics and beliefs. There was always a bad vibe in our home because of her. My grandma, uncles, and aunts had never shown me any affection. So, from the beginning, I had strange thoughts about other people since I assumed that everyone was the same. I was always at ease around her. I also had a few neighbourhood pals, so I spent the majority of my time playing with them. I had an issue with speaking ever since I was a toddler, and my words weren't clear. Other folks had a tough time understanding what I was conveying to them.

"Humans often find someone's disability as a way of their entertainment'.

I attended school, but the setting I found myself in was absolutely bizarre. Because I couldn't speak correctly because of the tongue problem, the youngsters teased me. I felt terrible; I went there hoping to make new acquaintances, but the outcome was utterly unexpected. This was the first time I questioned myself, and instead of developing new acquaintances, I began to disregard them. But in that class, there was a guy named Vibhu who was really humble and polite to me. He never made fun of me. I felt at ease with him, and we became great friends.

I began to like some aspects of my school life. I was not particularly gifted in the classroom. But the other students had always mistreated me because of my tongue problems and average study skills. But Vibhu was the only one who was kind and courteous to me. We used to visit one another's homes. Even his parents were so wonderful that they always treated and cared for me as if I were one of their own children. I was overjoyed since I had advanced to the following class.

My cousin was a guy by the name of Abhi. We had a close relationship. When I was four years old, I had an accident in which the mirror hit my forehead and caused an injury. When I totally passed out, my parents hurried me to the hospital. My mother, however, discovered that I had some pieces of the mirror stuck in my face when we got to the hospital. When they discovered my illness, the hospital's doctors were completely surprised. They performed an operation as soon as they brought me to the emergency room. By the grace of God, the procedure was successful. My entire face, though, was now bound up in bandages. After more than a month of healing, the day came when the doctor peeled off all the bandages covering my face. After such a long period, I was startled to see myself in the mirror and discover that my forehead was neatly lined with 38 stitches.

"I started to cry, and they thought I was kidding'.

It was a really terrible time for me since I knew that because of these marks, I was going to become the object of scorn. Even though I was aware that everything would proceed exactly as I had anticipated, I still went to school. And regrettably, that's exactly what took place. Everyone made fun of my marks, and as I saw them laughing at me, I became upset, and my eyes started to flood up with tears. For me, it was a wholly depressing and unpleasant experience. When I knew what was waiting for me at school, I couldn't help but hate myself for going there in the first place.

The guy I trusted the most, Abhay, joined in the laughter right then. He was the one in whom I had put my whole trust, and seeing him insult me broke my heart totally. When I got home, I told my mother everything that had happened at school. She calmed me and gave me comfort by saying that it was regrettably common for people to make fun of such things. She made it clear, though, that I shouldn't let their nasty actions cause me to lose faith in myself.

For the following 15 to 20 days, I skipped school. Then I went back to school after mentally preparing myself for the criticism. But then something very unexpected happened. My attention shifted to the same person who had been constantly making fun of me. I worked up the guts to talk to the teacher and tell her everything. Surprisingly, the teacher told me to ignore his offensive comments rather than discipline him. She urged me to keep my attention on the positive aspects of life and to shrug off his negative influences. It was quite difficult for me to face all of this criticism on my own because I was only 4 years old at the time.

"The worst thing about feelings is that, except for one, no one can understand them'.

Every single day was nearly as bad as hell for me. Every day, as I looked in the mirror, I wanted to get rid of those marks on my face because they made me feel so uneasy and anxious. I didn't talk to anyone during that time period. I didn't respond to those who made fun of me. But one thing I observed about my behaviour over time was that I became more self-conscious. I had been bullied by some of the students, but I never told my parents or anyone else about it. I despised my appearance because of the scars and marks, and my tongue problems prevented me from speaking to anyone. Simply put, I remained in that state for the entire following year. Because all of these thoughts were always circling through my head and I began to shun youngsters in my society, it had an impact on me in my day-to-day existence as well.

I wasn't good at studying, and there was a teacher in our school. She assumed that because I was so quiet and didn't seem interested in my studies, she didn't like me. She then began yelling at me about my grades and continuously tried to make me feel bad in the hopes that I would realise the importance of education. She was unaware of my insecurities, though I suppressed myself often because of them.

"Darkness doesn't exist; it's just an absence of light'.

She once called my parents to arrange a parent-teacher meeting, during which she told them everything about my classroom conduct. Her motivation to raise my academic achievement was sincere. However, not even my parents at the time understood what I was going through. My parents sent me to the extra classes for the first time as a result. They have always sought the best for me academically. My major worry, though, was usually the insecurities I was experiencing at the moment. Others may not have thought it was a big deal, but I felt like it was a nightmare.

But now, because of those extra classes, I have improved a little bit in my academic performance. My parents were happy that they no longer had to worry about my academic performance for the first time. I now began receiving good grades in exams, and the instructor who had previously disciplined me became a mentor to me. She gave me a lot of advice and supported me in my academic endeavours so that I could get better grades. I kept my fears a secret from her, but I did notice something remarkable: the other students stopped making fun of me. I even joined a group of 8–9 other pupils. All of a sudden, everyone became my close buddies. I can only say that it was the first time I actually relished my time at school. I started to feel a little better about myself.

2.

I WAS DIFFERENT FROM OTHERS

"We are social animals, but when someone tries to live with their own methods, society starts ignoring them'.

Television was a common medium at the time, where people used to watch movies, TV shows, and cartoons. I didn't find any interest in the movies or music that were shown on television, other than cartoons. When I used to see that kind of stuff, it used to make me feel quite unhappy and occasionally even angry. My parents described me as being very frustrated because of my unique behaviour. Even in my school, these topics were frequently discussed, but I was unable to relate to them.

I started to lose my place in such conversations as a result, because I had nothing to add. After a while, the group I had joined started to disregard me, and I once again felt alone. Watching cartoons, especially Tom & Jerry, gave me comfort. I recall watching it every day, and those were times of joy in my life. I delighted in being alone and in the pleasure of watching cartoons. Since it wasn't a very modern period.

I joined another group where there were two other boys. We formed a circle of our own and became close friends. We guys always discussed these performances and exchanged personal stories with one another. One day, my parents abruptly told us that we had to get out of the house right now. They appeared to be in a hurry and were tense. I asked them several times, but they never replied or offered an explanation. They made a decision that profoundly offended me, so I avoided them for a few days. The idea of leaving that place behind was difficult for me to accept because I had so many memories there.

"Hate only gives birth to the devil, and that devil creates trauma for others'.

Even though he never wanted to leave the house himself, my father eventually explained the situation to me. I was extremely shocked and terrified by the explanation he gave me. An aunt of mine had resided in our home. My father told me she used dark tactics to achieve her goals, and she was odd. I never warmed up to that woman. She attempted to murder our entire family using her sinister methods. The fact that she was responsible for my accident with the mirror, though, was the most stunning thing I learned.

After knowing this, I couldn't help but wonder what I had done wrong and how someone could have done this to me or to anyone else, and it utterly shattered me from the inside out. I've been forced to endure pain for the rest of my life as a result of someone else's evil deeds. I have nevertheless observed that I am no longer self-conscious about my scars and marks. I now had a strong dislike for that woman, which is another shift that had happened. I do, however, always manage to restrain my rage whenever my family brings her up.

"Scars are always there to remind us that we have a past'.

My parents used to hear spiritual bhajans when I was between three and four years old. I'd just realized a strange thing about myself. Whenever my father's listening to those devotional bhajans, it often brings back vivid recollections of my school days and particular incidents from that period. I had the sensation that I'd been transported back in time since I can vividly remember and repeat those events in great detail in my head. It felt like I was going back in time.

I discovered that the same thing was happening with both music and movies. When I listened to or watched movies or TV episodes that I had seen a few years earlier, I would be transported from the present to that particular era, which struck me as quite strange. It was extremely enjoyable at first, but after a while, it started to bother me

My brain could recognize and connect particular musical notes to memories. Whenever I went to temples or locations where bhajans were sung, I could feel the energy there and feel connected to it. It seems as though, because of those events, I have started to absolutely avoid watching cartoons, listening to music, and even watching movies. It had an uneasy feeling to it. But I never mentioned this to anyone since I thought it could give the wrong impression of who I am. I therefore made the decision to keep it a secret and merely declined to engage in any talk about such subjects. become etched in my mind on a profound level.

3.

CRICKET GAVE ME THAT OPPORTUNITY I WAS LOOKING FOR

"When we start to find joy in small things, We glow differently.'

I used to enjoy watching cricket on television and had always yearned to play. In our home, my father, brother, and I used to play cricket. I always attempted to play like Sachin Tendulkar since I was an admirer of him. I participated in the practice sessions for the cricket game that was permitted at our school.

I became a skilled batsman with sound technique as I improved in cricket. My brother, a cricketer who had received professional training, gave me invaluable advice and encouragement. I was chosen for the class cricket team, where I contributed significantly and played several great innings. It was the first time my peers had shown me admiration.

The following year, I was selected as the captain of my class team, and under my direction, we had success, winning several games. I not only got better academically as I got to the tenth grade, but I also got better at cricket. Some people were envious of my success because it was in two different areas of my life.

As time went on, my love for cricket grew, and I started to take it seriously. I grew close to the guys in my area, and we developed a solid friendship. In our neighbourhood, we hosted cricket competitions that were a success and well-liked by the locals. I then took the management of cricket competitions to a completely new level. I didn't let my father's dislike of me bother me much. I valued the leadership skills I had acquired through planning cricket competitions, and I was determined to keep them. I persisted in following my passion and maintaining my position as a leader in the cricket world despite my father's yelling at me for taking part in these activities.

4.

THE UNEXPECTED WHO BECAME A SPECIAL ONE

As the time passed, I started using social media. It was quite interesting because there were random people out there with whom I could talk. So I spent a lot of my time there, and I made several new friends. One day, I met a girl named Jasleen. She was from another city, but in a short period of time, we became close friends, and later on, we were in a relationship. Her father was a police inspector, so it was very difficult for her to maintain a healthy conversation with me.

But still, she tried her best, but one day her father got to know about our relationship, and her father called me and warned me not to call her again. And after a month of our immature relationship, we finally broke up. This incident didn't make any kind of impact on me because I wasn't serious about her; I knew that from the beginning. So I moved on without causing any emotional damage.

"Love not only makes us comfortable and happy; it actually completes us from the inside.'

Everything was going smoothly until the day I actually met a special someone. I had previously formed crushes on several different girls, but this time it seemed different. She had a somewhat "goon"-like character when I first met her on Facebook, which I found intriguing. We grew close, and as time passed, my affection for her intensified. I plucked up the guts and proposed to her , and happily, she said yes. She treated me tenderly and lovingly when our love story first started, almost like a child. Every second of it was fun for me. I adored her unconditionally, despite the fact that she was a slightly naive companion.

She was very open-minded, which was her best quality. When I was with her, I never felt like I was missing anything. She was the one who really made me whole. The things I loved the most were holding her hands. I thought I had everything I needed, and I was very happy. My goal in life was to build a balanced career at this point, and she constantly encouraged me to achieve my goals. She was there for me at all times. She was a part of me, and she made my world complete.

"The bad thing about the good moments is that they will never happen again.'

For a full year, things in our relationship were wonderful. I treasured countless moments with her, which I consider to be priceless. We gradually resembled the merging of two souls into one. We became even closer as a result of my ability to detect the sincerity of true love coming from her. Whenever I visited any temple, I never asked for anything for myself during that time. My only thoughts and prayers were for her pleasure and well-being. She then prayed for me in response. Her eyes were so deep, it felt like they were holding a depth of purity. I couldn't control myself. I always adore those eyes. They had a compelling appeal that prevented me from becoming even the slightest bit bored over the entire day.

5.

I EXPERIENCED SOMETHING UNIQUE AND BEAUTIFUL

"We discover ourselves regularly by exploring new things.'

I'd been in a relationship for more than a year, and during that time, I cut ties with Cricket and the majority of my friends. I had a sense of fulfillment in my life. However, because it was an era of the internet, my only experience with the internet was through social networking sites.

We finally installed WiFi in our home, so I started browsing the web. I discovered YouTube throughout my research, which was a new medium to me. I looked for random things because I had no interest in music or movies. I did, however, come across something unexpected and pleasant when I looked up the cartoons I watched as a kid. It was a special experience for me because I never imagined having independent access to so many beloved cartoons.

After a few days, I by chance stumbled onto Michael Jackson's music. I had no prior awareness of this individual or his music, but I had heard about him as a result of his shocking passing in 2009. "Black or White" by Michael Jackson was the first music I heard, and it utterly fascinated me. It was undoubtedly unique. Everything about the song—music, lyrics, and videography—was flawless. I was practically hypnotised by the compelling influence it had on me as I lost myself in the enchanting universe of Michael Jackson's skill.

"Music is nature's biggest gift to us. It can motivate us, trigger our emotions, and make us cry and be happy. So be careful about your music.'

My interest in Michael Jackson's songs grew stronger as I learned more about his music. Since every pulse and tune made my body feel alive, I yearned to dance like him. We had no recollection of dancing together, so when my partner found out that I was listening to music, she was surprised. She did, however, respect my connection to music and my newfound happiness. Even though I tried to sing for her, my voice didn't do the song any credit, but it didn't matter because the emotions the music evoked in me were sufficient to express my feelings.

Now I wanted to learn dance, and my partner first thought I was insane and didn't understand why I wanted to pursue dance when I told her that I wanted to learn it. However, I was able to persuade her of my sincerity and love through conversation and explanation. She finally gave in and approved my plan to take dancing lessons.

My parents' dismissal of my passion for dance wounded my heart, but I was determined to pursue it no matter what. After a few days, I read an ad about dance courses in the newspaper. I decided to enrol in those classes on my own without notifying anyone.

"Nothing can stop us when we have the right intentions for something.'

I had a wave of nervousness and excitement on the day of the lesson. Everyone there appeared to be extremely gifted and well-trained. I was so overcome with self-doubt that I almost lost it. I eventually controlled my agitation, though, and went up to the instructor. I showed an interest in learning, but I had no idea what he was talking about when he inquired about my musical tastes and preferred dancing styles. I had no knowledge of dancing or musical terms. I was at a loss for words at the time and only said, "Sir, I just want to dance like Michael Jackson.

I was politely told by the senior teacher, who was grinning at me, that I would need to work very hard if I wanted to dance like him. He assumed the responsibility of instructing me directly. He concentrated on improving my sense of rhythm and beat recognition throughout our first classes. He introduced me to some fundamental dancing steps and told me about three different kinds of patterns. taught me some fundamental dance steps. I occasionally found it difficult to follow the directions because they were tied to a popular Hindi song that I had never heard before. The instructor just emphasised the value of cultivating my own musical sense of rhythm while encouraging me to identify the beat on my own.

"We don't dance; we just feel the music and relate ourselves to it.'

The other day, I successfully completed some of the dance moves after finally learning the technique for identifying the rhythms. Even the teacher saw how far I had come. After some days, I told my folks about my accomplishments after feeling proud of myself. They finally consented to assist me in pursuing my passion for dance after repeated petitions and nagging.

6.

I NEVER KNEW THAT ONE WAS ACTUALLY FOR ME

"With the right approach and perspective, we can do everything.'

I had a burning desire to dance and committed to working hard every day. I knew exactly what I wanted to do. I observed development and improvement every day. I improved as a dancer in the next few months by learning the techniques with more assurance and grace. I had to take a break from my dance courses as my board examinations got closer so that I could concentrate on my studies. My thoughts, however, were more focused on dance than on my tests. All I wanted was for the examinations to be completed so that I could go back to my dance classes, so I wasn't really serious about studying.

I simply spent a few hours a day studying and gave it a fair effort. The tests eventually came and were over in a few days. Even though I wasn't at the height of my devotion and focus, I was still able to finish them. I went back to my dance classes knowing exactly what I wanted to accomplish. I was tenacious and laser-focused. In order to guarantee that my motions were clean and accurate, I made it a point to coordinate with the more experienced dancers. My teacher was impressed by my devotion and effort because I was efficient with my time during sessions.

"Devotion is just a combination of dedication and consistency towards your higher self.'

I worked hard to refine and enhance my dancing abilities. I had learned most of Michael Jackson's dancing movements by this point. I had gotten really good at copying his mannerisms. I showed my teacher my movement repertoire, and he was really impressed. He urged me to concentrate on this particular dance form and develop my abilities. I put in even more practice time, and as the days went by, my moves got better.

I made the decision to prepare a performance for myself with my newly acquired confidence, thinking that I would soon get the chance to demonstrate my abilities. By chance, a group from another state came to visit our studio in the month of September. They were organising a gathering in our city, opening up the possibility for me to play. Our teacher revealed the lineup of artists the following day. Unfortunately, I didn't see my name on the list, which disappointed me. My teacher clarified that his reputation was at stake, so he couldn't take any chances.

"We get opportunities every single day, so be careful and aware. We never know what's or who's next'.

After a few days, I learned that some of the performers on the initial lineup were no longer available for the occasion. When my sir called, he inquired as to whether I was at ease and confident enough to take their place. I gave him a prompt yes over the phone when he requested it without any hesitation. He asked me to prepare a performance skit for the event because he wanted to see it beforehand. I put a lot of effort into the skit, concentrating on doing Michael Jackson's impersonation. I went to my teacher and presented him with the performance after it was over. He seems appreciative of my efforts while also expressing some apprehensions. He wasn't sure if I could perform or not, so adding my name to the list was a bit of a chance for him.

A total of 35–40 artists were set to perform that night when the festival got underway. I had never performed in the solo category before, so I was anxious as I waited my turn. Our teacher convened a meeting with us in the midst of the incident to stress the significance of the situation and how his reputation was on the line. In our group, my performance was slated to be the ninth act.

I heard the host call my name, indicating that it was my turn to take the stage, and I was both excited and uneasy. The platform seemed larger than I expected, with over 1000 people present, and I felt a wave of fear almost overpower me. I was able to collect myself, though, and get ready for my performance. I found myself going temporarily blank as the music began to play and losing track of why I was on that stage. The music abruptly halted as a result of an unanticipated sound system malfunction.

"When we lose our confidence, we not only fall, we just accept our fate at that time.'

The technical problem was rectified after around 15 minutes. I used this time to go to the bathroom and try to calm myself down as much as I could. When I got back to the performance space, I saw that our teacher was upset with me because I had almost ruined everything. He was disappointed, but he didn't express it because he didn't want me to lose faith in him. I just wanted to make him happy.

I felt more at ease and in charge as I re-entered the stage. As soon as the music began again, I gave it everything I had and did my absolute best. You gave it your best, and may God bless you, as my teacher stated after I submitted my work. His words meant a lot to me, and I felt glad that I had somewhat atoned for my actions. As the results were released, it was crunch time. Our team won third place in the group category, and we were ecstatic and appreciative of that accomplishment. But when the emcee announced my name as the runner-up in the solo category, it was the most unexpected and strange event of my life. I could hardly believe what I was seeing before my eyes because it felt like a dream. My fellow dancers and the entire studio were startled and thrilled for me.

"Your karma will never let you down.'

Still in shock, I approached the platform, where I was given a trophy and a check for 25,000 rupees. The monetary award was a pleasant surprise, even though I was not aware of it previously. Nevertheless, there was a hint of regret mixed in with the pleasure. Due to my anxiety, I had not invited my partner and family to share in this memorable occasion. Being separated from my loved ones diminished the excitement of winning a medal or obtaining a position, which was a first for me.

I was experiencing a variety of emotions, but I was able to gather myself and go back to my teacher. He was ecstatic and emphasised how surprised he was by my outcome. I shared in his joy and expressed my gratitude for his teachings and encouragement during my dance career. I felt so guilty that my family wasn't there to see me succeed when I got home because of this. My mother advised me to retain the money I received and not tell my brother and father about it because they weren't home at the time. She wished for me to possess something as a memento of my success.

I felt a range of emotions in response to her compassion and encouragement, including gratitude for her support as well as a wish for my family's presence at that pivotal time. But I appreciated my mother's kind gesture and held the memory of my success dear to my heart.

"Life seems like a dream when we achieve unexpected things.'

Naina was obviously disappointed that she couldn't be present to witness such a significant milestone in my life when I told her about the entire incident. She expressed her disappointment by being silent and refraining from speaking to me for the following few days.

Naina, though, saw things differently. She felt that I had already accomplished my objective and that it was now time for me to concentrate on my study. She urged me to give up dancing in favor of my academic goals. We felt tension between us as we discussed our ambitions and future goals as a result of this difference in viewpoint.

"When something touches our soul through its appearance, we create another extension of ourselves.'

I noticed that I was becoming disinterested in studying after I decided to attend college for a Bachelor of Arts degree. It devolved into a pursuit that was only done to earn a degree. I once went with my dance friend to a required musical class. I was mesmerised by the students' singing and instrument playing as soon as I entered the classroom. Despite the fact that I didn't know much about music at the time, it was a unique experience for me. I had a burning urge to go on their musical adventure with them. We were there for about 25 minutes, and throughout that time, I was completely engrossed in the delight of the music, especially their English songs and rhymes.

The tunes and harmonies carried on in my head when I got home. I couldn't help but attempt to rhyme in time with the music playing in my head. I was curious about this newfound love, so I looked into musical instruments. I was drawn to the piano and felt a strong urge to learn how to play it. As my attention moved from dancing to wanting to join this musical ensemble, this caused uncertainty in my head.

I was excited to start my musical journey, so the very next day I went to the store and bought a Casio piano for myself. I decided to enroll in classes at the musical institute without telling anyone. I didn't tell anyone, not even my family or Naina, about this.

"We do not get blinded by our eyes; we get blinded by our minds'.

My mother grew upset when I finally told her the news because she could see that I was clearly heading in an uncertain direction. Naina's response was no different; when she learned about my choice, she yelled at me. I was scared and worried that I would lose her because of my newfound interest. I felt guilty for not taking Naina's feelings into account and apologised to her, but she didn't seem to care.

I persisted in going to my music lessons, eventually sharpening my attention and letting my newfound enthusiasm dominate me. I started to become a little self-centered and put my interests before other commitments. I soon picked up the fundamentals of music and started to devote a large amount of my attention to it. The musical group I joined and the music teacher both exhibited really sincere behaviour.

Krish, one of the group members, encouraged me to try singing as well. I decided to enrol in vocal lessons despite my anxiety due to past worries regarding my tongue problems. Over time, I developed my vocal skills and gained more self-assurance.

"There is a big difference between getting fascinated and being dedicated or passionate about something'.

One day I got a phone call from my college, and they wanted to see me with my father. Me and my father went to the college, and the principal shared my attendance report with my father. My father was upset with me after learning of my attendance. The principal warned me and said he would punish me if I didn't focus on my studies again. Next month, there were going to be semester exams, and my father was very upset with me because of my college reports. My father warned me and said he wants good results in the semester exams. So I took a break from everything and started focusing on my studies. When the exams came, I performed very well in those exams. As the exams got over, I rejoined my dance and musical classes again.

A significant Bollywood film was scheduled for release in December, around the time of the Christmas and New Year festivities. In our city, an event company planned a large event to advertise the movie. My dance instructor got in touch with me at this time. He asked me to perform, so I practised three songs that included singing and dancing for the occasion.

"Whenever we put all of our efforts into something, we not only get the best result, but we also become an inspiration to others.'

I was excited to have the chance to perform and show off my singing and dancing skills, so I started working hard to get ready. I experienced a resurgence of motivation and drive, and I was ready to establish myself on a greater stage. I had no idea that this performance would mark a significant turning point in my life.

I remained steadfast in my commitment and persisted despite my dance teacher's initial doubts about fusing singing and dancing. I argued that I would only perform if I could combine my abilities in singing and dance. My dance instructor finally gave in to my request.

On the day of the event, a number of artists entered the stage and displayed their distinctive talents. As soon as my name was called, I entered the stage while carrying a wireless microphone. I launched into my performance as the music started, flawlessly fusing singing and dancing.

I was surprised and delighted to see how enthusiastically the audience responded. The audience erupted in jubilation as soon as I started singing. I put my entire being into the performance, putting on a fantastic show. I won first place after the judges acknowledged my talent and dubbed me the "First Dancing Musician of Amritsar.

In that moment, I felt triumphant and validated, knowing that I had made the right choice to pursue both singing and dance. I was so happy and grateful for the acknowledgement that it inspired me to keep pushing the envelope and improving as a dance musician.

"The day when we are able to reward ourselves with pride is the day we finally understand the value of our efforts.'

7.

EVERYTHING WENT AGAINST ME

"The unique thing about bad experiences is that we will never notice them while suffering.'

Everything was going well, but every time I practised my vocals or jammed, I felt a scratchy sensation in my throat. I initially disregarded this, but as time went on, it grew more significant. Along with the itch, I also experienced some throat soreness and a slight sense of exhaustion. When I discussed this with my music teacher, he speculated that I might have a throat infection and encouraged me to see a doctor as soon as possible. I went to the doctor since he and our family had a good relationship, and I told him everything that was happening. He gave me some medication and said I should take a few days off from vocal practice. I took his recommendations to heart, and things started to look up. But a few days later, the same problems returned, and this time they were far worse. My throat started to swell, and I could immediately tell that something was amiss.

I returned to the doctor and described what had transpired. This time, the doctor gave me some stronger prescriptions and suggested that I take a little sabbatical. Since I hadn't notified my family or my partner about this scenario, I was a little concerned for my health. They would adamantly demand that I stop doing everything and focus on taking care of my health, but I didn't want to give up under any circumstances.

I persisted in attending my dance classes despite everything. But this time I felt a weakness in my body and had some trouble breathing. I made the decision to leave the studio and go home because I couldn't complete my practices correctly. I was worried about everything that was happening to me. I returned to the doctor and laid out everything. He gave me reassurance that it was a side effect of the potent medications I had been taking and told me not to be alarmed. He advised me to take a longer break from my activities so that my body could recuperate more fully.

I decided to stop taking dancing classes as well since I wanted to focus my attention on getting my body ready for good training. But Naina insisted that I tell her everything because she thought I was concealing something from her. I did my best to keep it a secret, but eventually I told her everything. She expressed a wish to speak with me and address it in person. She was very clear when we first met that she wanted me to stop doing all of these things. She seemed to ignore my sentiments about my passion this time, so I was surprised by her seriousness. I became utterly perplexed as a result of this, since I didn't want to give up my desire but also didn't want to lose her.

I became aware that I had completely disregarded my studies as the college examinations of 2nd semester got closer. I was facing penalties like fines and a 70–80% drop in my attendance record because I hadn't gone to a single lecture in the last few months. I came to the conclusion that I would stop studying without telling anyone.

My family was furious when they learned about my choice, especially my father. I had to go carefully through the situation, expressing my regret and making an effort to calm their ire. Naina, however, erupted in a fit of rage when she found out about my decision. She threatened to leave me if I didn't get rid of these activities as quickly as possible.

"Try to differentiate between a constructive and destructive path; our one mistake will lead us to the failure side.'

I kept going to my dancing classes and a few vocal lessons despite my frail physique and damaged vocal cords. However, I was unable to provide my full effort. I turned my attention to my vocals after realising that singing properly was my top priority. This time, I worked really hard, and I even started taking medications to protect myself against allergies. Eventually, it was successful, and I was once again able to sing. However, I became aware of my body's weight loss. Others started to notice it after a month as well. Following my doctor's recommendation to abstain from dairy products for a few days, which I had already been doing, led to this weight loss.

The first semester result came, and I got to know that I was in the 3rd position in my class. I already left my studies, and now this result meant nothing to me. I notified my family, and they got upset with me.

My dance instructor called me one day and inquired why I hadn't been coming to class, saying he wanted to see me. I went to the dance studio and told him all about it. He gave me the advice to give my dance my undivided attention, just like I used to. I continued to practise, but during one session I unintentionally passed out and fell to the ground. Thank goodness, those around me sprang into action, and I came to. I made it back home even though I felt disoriented. The following day, I went to see my doctor once more and explained everything. This time, he mandated that I take a protracted sabbatical and prescribed some extra drugs. I opted not to tell my family or Naina about this, but I did talk about it with my friends. My body felt like it was under a tremendous amount of stress, and I had numerous nights where I couldn't sleep. The events that were taking place entirely occupied my mind.

I started having other health problems, like a fever, and my body wasn't digesting correctly because I couldn't sleep. I asked a friend of mine who worked in medicine if he could get me some sleeping pills so I could get some rest. I also didn't talk about this with my doctor. In order to achieve quality sleep, I started taking sleeping medications, and I developed an addiction to them. I eventually needed medication to fall asleep. My entire body weakened as a result, and I dropped about 8-9 kg of body weight in a short period of time. The people surrounding me observed this change. My relationship with Naina was getting worse every day, to the point that she stopped communicating with me for a month. She was the only one I felt at ease with; therefore, this had a big impact on me.

I developed a complete addiction and couldn't go to sleep without taking medication. My other friends were informed of this knowledge by the friend who had given me the tablets, and they then told everyone else. When Naina learned, she called me and asked to meet. When I went to see her, she was crying this time because of how I was feeling. She nearly pleaded with me to stop using these medications, but I ignored her since I always thought everything would turn out okay in the end. She yelled at me as I became agitated, and I lost control. I ultimately struck her and cursed at her. She told me to stop contacting her before she left.

"A person with a broken heart sees the world from a different perspective. Everything is just broken for him or her.'

Perhaps the worst day of my life was that one. I knew something was really wrong, but I was unable to respond to what had happened. My heart was racing so hard that my entire body shook. My heart felt like it was breaking. My folks were already aware of what I had been going through when I got home, I learned. This time, they were all acting really serious. I wanted to say something, but I couldn't because of what I had done to Naina. I was unable to speak a single word. I went to my bedroom and sobbed all night. I was thinking about committing suicide for the first time because I was unable to control everything going on at the time.

But I wasn't not sure how I exercised self-control and refrained from doing that. I made an effort to get in touch with her, but she didn't reply. This particular information was mentally torturing me. I just wanted to talk to her, so I just wanted her to be there. I was so highly reliant on the tablets that I would sometimes take two or three. I started avoiding people and turned off my phone entirely, cutting off any contact with the outside world.

8.

The BETRAYAL

"Betrayal never comes from your enemy; it always comes from the person we trust the most.'

My family was now really worried about how I was doing. They made the choice to take me to a different medical professional who focused on psychological and health issues. I gave him all the information, and he became my therapist. He also suggested that I seek the advice of an ENT specialist for my medical care. After a week of seeing me, the ENT expert sent in his final report. When I discovered that my condition was actually a minor but significant diaphragm ailment, I was astounded. My former doctor's recommended drugs had nothing to do with it. These drugs merely offered short-term respite; they didn't deal with the fundamental issue.

The ENT expert broke the heartbreaking news that I would never be able to sing again because of a diaphragm problem, which also explained why I had tongue problems from birth. When I learned of this, I was devastated. I suddenly found myself stunned and at a loss for words. I learned the next day that Naina intended to get married that same year. Negative ideas about ending my life came to me for the second time. I tried to get in touch with Naina, but she didn't respond very well. You're not the same person I once knew, she said. You are now an entirely different person—selfish, egotistical, and devoid of compassion for anyone. Such a person is not someone I can spend my life with. I apologise.

"Expectations always hurts

Unexpected things always surprised'.

I felt absolutely lost and without a purpose in life at this point. My doctor had practically squandered a year of my life with worthless drugs, and I felt betrayed by him. I made the decision to put dancing and music aside. I spent most of my time alone because I had no one to confide in. My sadness was increased by the perception that my diaphragm problem was unfixable.

Like when I was a child, I found myself living a life without music and friends once more. Self-doubts started to appear, and I started to feel aimless and lost. I was unsure of what I was actually doing with my life for the first time.

Naina married another individual as time went on. I was unable to speak during that time since I was dreaming about a life with her. But because of everything that was going on, I ended up in the worst situation I could have ever imagined. That night, I took around six sleeping pills with the thought of ending my life, but my brain was tired and it didn't work. I was in charge, even though it felt like I had lost half of myself.

During this time, I wasn't able to move on from Naina because her memories still haunt me, and it was very difficult for me.

There was a friend of mine in college; we were friends and used to communicate through Facebook. She had no idea what was going on in my life, and one day I received a text from her side. We had a good conversation. I started spending my time with her, and she was showing her interest in and feelings for me. I wanted to forget about Naina and have a new love life.

So I started showing my own interest in her, and one day she expressed her feelings, and I accepted her proposal. But from inside, I was just pretending, and she thought I was in love with her. She took care of me like I was everything to her. I shared everything with her about what was happening with me at that time, and she accepted everything. She gave her best for my betterment, but still, I wasn't able to recover because all of those things were killing me from inside, and it was like an infinity loop for me. After some days, I realised I had no feelings for her and was just playing with her. I made my decision and told her everything. We were on the call, and she cried like she had lost everything because I broke her trust. She asked me why I did this to her, and I had nothing to say at that time. I apologised for my actions, but she just left me without saying anything.

Her crying voice was stuck in my head now because it was the first time I had betrayed someone for my own benefit. I knew that it would be difficult for me to face all these things, so I started taking more sleeping pills as part of my daily routine and spent most of my time sleeping. I tried to contact her multiple times, but she didn't respond to any of my calls or texts. Now I realised I had lost another good person in my life, and it was very difficult for me to accept that. During these days, one of my friend's Facebook accounts got hacked by someone, and that person spread rumours about my death.

It was around 1 a.m., and my family received multiple calls from our relatives and friends about this situation, but we were unaware of it. Even that person revealed everything about my condition, and now everyone was aware of what was happening with me. This moment was very embarrassing for my family, and my father stopped talking to me after that day. My bond with my family was getting worse day by day.

One of my friends who used to dance with me had contacted me, and he said he was aware of everything and wanted to see me. He was the kind of person who had good connections with mafia-type people, and he was like that person. We were good friends, so he wanted to help me, but because of his goon-type aura, I had no control over him. He asked me plenty of things, but I wasn't able to answer any of his questions because I wasn't feeling comfortable. I wanted to leave, but he didn't let me leave, and he said he had something for me, like a surprise gift.

I had no idea what he was talking about, so I stayed there. It was almost around 9 p.m., and he said we had to leave that place, so he booked a room at some hotel, but I wasn't comfortable with that, so I couldn't say this to him. We went there, and he ordered some food for us, and we started a good conversation. Now it was around 11 p.m. I got calls from my family, but he didn't let me leave; he almost forced me to stay there.

Suddenly, he got a call from someone, and he told someone about our hotel, and now I was feeling so uncomfortable because I had no idea who was on the other side. A girl came up to our room, and my friend said it was a surprise gift for me from him. She was a call girl. And I almost went blank because I had no idea what was going on there. I was about to leave, but my friend yelled at me. He said something to that girl, and he left that room. Now it was me and that girl. She tried her best to make me comfortable, but I felt so anxious that she noticed that I was getting nervous. She was getting rude to me because of my behaviour. She tried to talk, but I wasn't able to speak a single word.

She was about to leave, and I started crying like a little kid, and seeing me like this made her confused. She came to me and asked me how I was feeling, but I was just crying. She gave me water and calmed me down. After some time, I got normal, and she was just looking at me with surprise. She asked me what happened to me, and I told her everything about what I was going through. She was just listening to me and didn't question me for once. Somehow, by telling her everything, it made me so relaxed that I felt like I had survived everything. I went to the washroom for a bath and took a shower, and I felt like I was in heaven for a while.

But as I came out of the washroom, I noticed that the girl wasn't there. I was a little bit shocked to see that, and when I asked the receptionist about that girl, he said she left the hotel a few minutes ago. I called my friend and informed him. I went back to the room and slept for a few hours. After a long time, I slept without any pills.

9.

SPIRITUALITY WAS SOMETHING GOOD

"The whole world depends on hope.

And hope begins with us.'

Now was the time when I had lost everything, like my bond with my family, my partner, my finances, and my health, and I didn't know what to do with my life.

Even my face started looking so dull, like I had lost all of my shine. I determined that I would overcome all of these difficulties and work to resume living a regular life. I had, however, grown distant from my loved ones and alienated from everything throughout this period. I looked for a solution on my own since I felt unsteady psychologically and physically. I started looking for solutions online. After a few days of searching, I came upon something called spirituality/meditation. I started learning more about its teachings since it struck me as a sincere and uplifting idea.

Due to my renewed interest, I came upon Instagram, a distinctive platform that stood out from the others I had used. I mostly looked up spirituality-related subjects on Instagram. One day, I received a message from a commenter who identified themselves as a spiritual teacher and asked to speak with me.

I started a chat with this person because, to me, they initially seemed to be something of a wizard. He amazed me by describing several facets of my life with great accuracy just by looking at my face. It completely shocked me. I was intrigued by his skills, so I asked him to teach me some spiritual techniques that would aid me in my quest for self-healing. He agreed to do it, but only if I gave them access to my whole daily schedule and all of my possessions. I hesitated, but I consented to their request. He then started teaching me various techniques like reiki energy, aura control, and meditation. These rituals were difficult for me to perform at first, but with time and effort, I began to understand them and started incorporating some of them into my everyday routine.

"Trust the universe with your full faith, and the universe will work for you.'

My health started to show a few modest changes, and the depression that had engulfed me started to lift. The real game-changer for me, though, was learning about the power of Reiki energy. It took me to a totally new world. I discovered how to manage my aura and how to feel other people's energy just by watching them. It evolved into a routine that helped me deal with small wounds and reduce discomfort. Even though I still lacked the self-assurance to face the world, I made the decision to work online as a way to rebuild myself.

I was hired by an online company, where my duties included gathering and providing data. It turned out to be a rewarding career that also offered a good salary, allowing me to autonomously handle my finances. I was happy because my life was focused on my job, my spiritual development, and my mentor. I still had a small amount of musical and dance-related interest, but I managed to keep my emotions in check. My health started to get a little better over time, and I started to feel better overall.

"When we make our growth our first priority, we grow differently.'

I started to experience a lot of strange things. I could sense and perceive everything more acutely, including emotions. I learned that I was capable of face-reading and even had the power to heal other people. My mentor cautioned me against utilising this healing talent on others, though, because I wasn't yet prepared for such a rite. Even though I had recovered from my depression, I continued to feel guilty about the prior mistakes I had made. This made it difficult for me to re-enter the world. I consequently decided to prioritise my psychological development and healing and forego physical meetups for a while.

I improved in confidence and health every day. The things that used to haunt me no longer had the same impact on me. I went through a lot of experiences during that time that no normal person could ever understand. My dreams were under my control, and I could create them. My entire family felt some sort of uplifting energy coming from me. They consistently said that, while they couldn't see it, they could sense a different kind of energy. I'm no longer dependent on sleeping drugs, and my addiction has been treated. I began seeing my friends and family.

10.

THE CONCEPT OF PARALLEL REALITY

"When we understand the power of spirituality, we only need ourselves for our own betterment.'

My spiritual fortitude strengthened with time, and my mentor and I nearly reached parity in our devotion to spirituality. Even though I still had a lot of respect for my guru, I felt drawn to delve even further into the spiritual world. In an effort to further my own education, I once again resorted to the internet. I discovered telepathy, a skill that helped me communicate with those who understood Reiki energy. My tutor was shocked by this talent.

My study took me to the most sinister parts of the internet, where I came across disturbing and illegal rituals connected to an occult sect. I faced a lot of darkness, but I didn't let it stop me from exploring. I chose to disassociate myself from those activities and continue my studies in other areas since I realised the rituals I discovered were really sinister and unethical. I learned several horrible facts about the world throughout this. I was completely shocked to see that this technique was used by the most powerful people for their own benefits, and it was quite dark. Even all those major events that happened in human history were done by this technique, but using this technique at its very best. There were kinds of rituals that were too dark, and there were communities and societies that actually performed this technique, and by using this technique, they actually controlled the whole world. From politicians to artists to historical figures, all of them are part of this thing. It was a big surprise for me that normal people like us have no idea that we are just living in simulation.

"The most powerful tool in the world is our mind. The day humans understand its true potential, we will discover those things we can't even imagine.'

I came upon the idea of "parallel reality," which I found to be both dark and unsettling. I was willing to investigate it further because it agreed with my ethical principles, despite any risks. I started studying this technique deeply, and the things I found there were disturbing. By using this method, we can live in the real world while creating a parallel universe that exists only in our brains. The ability to depict two different characters/realities at once was an essential component of this technique. In essence, it required brain-tricking to implant a notion into the mind, opening the door to a variety of possibilities, such as curing serious illnesses through self-directed methods, But most of the time, this technique was used for planning an event, like making others believe that a particular event was going to happen in the near future. It did, however, carry considerable danger and potential repercussions.

A key component of this technique was the idea of distinguishing between the real world and the made-up parallel world. I was conscious that there would be hazards of misunderstanding and losing touch with reality if I couldn't adequately absorb and understand this concept. However, I had a strong desire to get past the diaphragm problem, so I started off by studying and doing this ritual at the base level.

"We will always fail until our last breath because our next attempt will always be considered a successor to the previous one.'

The technique was at first incredibly confusing, and that was the first thing I noticed. It appeared to be normal while I was reading, but when I tried to put this strategy into practice, I utterly failed the first few times because switching between two characters was almost like confusing myself.

The worst part was that I was unable to discuss this with anyone; not even my mentor knew what I was up to. So I made up a persona in my head who was healthy, and somehow I was able to convince myself that I was also healthy. I did this by creating my own world where I was fully healthy and had no history like this, using the lucid dreaming technique. To put it simply, I hypnotised myself in order to alter my beliefs.

The issue now was that, aside from me, everyone was aware of my condition. So, this method wouldn't work because I was aware of the harm I was causing myself. I need everyone to think I didn't have any health difficulties if I want to make this happen.

So, I found it too challenging. I had been practising for a few days at this point, and I had observed that my body had improved. But this time, I pretended as if nothing had ever happened to me before. Actually, there was no longer any pain or difficulty breathing as a result of it. The issue, though, was that if my entire family and friends learned that I had resumed my vocal training, they would all turn against me.

I now require something fresh in order to exert mental control over others and successfully implant that notion. It took me more than three months to figure out the answer, and I discovered that answer in the Bible. The Bible contained prophecies made by Jesus regarding the future, and I realised that everything was transpiring exactly as it had been described. I was astonished and relieved all at once that I had discovered the answer. I never discussed anything negative about myself with others, and whenever they tried to discuss my history in discussion, I would correct them. I always talked to them about those potential outcomes that never materialised. They unexpectedly began to believe what I told them. I always rebuffed attempts to start a dialogue about those topics, even within my own family.

I was only anticipating the day when the doctor would provide me with official proof. I therefore waited for approximately 6-7 weeks, telling myself daily that I had a great past. Then, by some miracle, I was no longer afflicted by that illness. Thankfully, nothing negative happened to me while I was attending some vocal sessions. With the exception of my mentor, I kept this to myself. Now, everyone assumed that I was in perfect condition and had no significant medical difficulties. But with time, my perception of myself also became entirely brainwashed, as evidenced by the fact that there were occasions when I couldn't tell the difference between the actual world and my dreams.

11.

THE GAME CHANGER

Now that I was clear about what my vision is and what I wanted to accomplish, I had started doing extensive study on that ritual, concentrating on the positive examples. I observed that my body comprehended everything I tried to do with it, which felt like a miracle to me. To prevent people from discussing what happened in the past, I avoided people from my past and made new friends. I was aware that it was a self-centred action, but I couldn't help it.

It was now time to make a comeback. I posted some piano covers at that time to my social media accounts, and I soon got a call from a band in search of a pianist. By God's goodness, I was chosen during the audition I attended. I joined a band, and we performed some good shows. I was quite confident about my health too and wanted to make a comeback as a singer.

There was a friend of mine, and from the last few days on, he was behaving very weirdly, and I noticed him at first sight. I figured out that something awful had happened to him, so I went to him and talked to him about his condition. He talked about his break-up story, and he was in huge pain. I couldn't see him in that condition, so I performed my healing technique on him. Within a few days, he recovered from his trauma and started living his life normally, and I was so happy to see that because I healed someone.

I shared this incident with my mentor, but he yelled at me because, according to him, I shouldn't have healed someone because I didn't know about this technique properly. Now my friend's negative energy was living within me, and it will affect me. Everything was going OK until I ate some fruits at home one day without cleaning them, exposing them to pesticides. My blood pressure fell after eating one of them, and I puked it all up. I started to shiver, though, and collapsed to the ground.

My mother called my brother and father when she was at home. I was taken to the hospital, where I spent the following three days as an inpatient. I eventually returned home. I was bedridden for the entire 25 days I received medical care.

The fact that the chemicals had damaged my diaphragm muscle was the worst news I had heard. I had pain in the muscles in my stomach whenever I attempted to sing. I had already diligently recovered from the prior circumstances, but now I couldn't heal myself using the same procedure, so I had no idea what to do. So that external energy wouldn't affect me any longer, I made the decision to keep this information a secret from everyone and took a sabbatical from my vocal practice. I wanted my body to recover organically.

I re-joined my band as the pianist in 2020, and we played a few events. But because of the coronavirus outbreak and subsequent global lockdown, I had to stay at home nonstop. I started putting my health and spirituality back at the forefront since I felt that it was the ideal time for recovery. But despite my best efforts this time, I was unable to produce the anticipated outcomes. I started to worry, but I kept practising. I also welcomed a lot of new people into my life during this period. I made some new friends who were unaware of my background. Despite the fact that I never revealed anything to them and instead made up a story about myself, I was still able to forge close relationships with them.

The lockdown eventually ended as time went on, and it was time to go back to the market and perform once more. The unanticipated lockdown, however, had drastically altered the market and had a big effect on the economics of the nation. As a result, the sum we were about to get was significantly less than what we had previously gotten. Members of my band decided to quit the group and look for employment in other industries. Without a degree, I was unable to obtain employment, and even the freelance work I had been doing had stopped. I didn't know where my life was going. I nevertheless continued my vocal practice with the goal of becoming the main vocalist of a brand new band. I decided to disregard the diaphragm pain I was dealing with everyday.

I got myself ready for a comeback, but after a few days, I started to feel terrible stomach aches. I went to the doctor and mentioned my concerns because I was worried about this. The doctor checked the location and ran a scan that was directed just at that spot. The doctor told me that a particular portion had suffered some harm as a result of the food poisoning problem. He urged me to wait for it to heal naturally and to refrain from singing during that period, as it would hinder the muscle's healing. Now, because of food poisoning, my body almost lost half of its weight, and as a result, I almost became like a skeleton. Now it was the first time I felt depressed because of my physical appearance, and at that time my body was around 37–38 kg. I made a decision and sold out my piano and other musical gadgets. I just wanted to take a break from everything. I sell everything at a very low price. Selling all of those gadgets made me a little bit upset because, after dance, I was almost out of music now.

There was a marriage occasion for my cousin during the following week. I was a little bit excited because I was devastated by my relatives' world, and after a long time, I was going to meet them. I went there, and the reaction I got from them was quite unexpected; some of them didn't recognize me. Each and every single individual asked me the same question about my health because I had lost my body weight, which actually affected my confidence level too. I stayed quiet and wanted to leave that place, but somehow I managed to do so by giving some random reason. From younger to elder, everyone was giving their own advice, and I was just listening to each of them and saying nothing, but in my mind, it actually crushed my soul. I had some expectations, like a warm welcome from them, but I just got sympathy. The lesson I learned was the value of a healthy person. For the next few days, this whole incident got stuck in my mind.

12.

CHOOSING PHILOSOPHY WAS A GOOD DECISION

While waiting for my diaphragm muscle to heal, I opted to join my family business and began studying philosophy because I felt like I had exhausted all singing-related opportunities. It was terribly boring at first, but as I submerged myself in it more, I started to get genuinely interested in the topic.

For me, this new enterprise represented a completely new universe. I was greatly inspired by the intelligence of the giants who lived throughout the planet, since they held an astounding level of knowledge comparable to that of the gods. I spent my spare time reading books and researching the fields of human psychology and philosophy in an effort to better grasp these interesting topics.

I not only experienced personal progress, but I also started offering advice to other people. I realised that I had grown to have a great sense of empathy for people's feelings and the suffering brought on by failures in their lives. I really like my work in this field. People found me on a number of my social media profiles, looking for answers to their concerns. I would carefully record their worries while I listened to them and then research the issues at hand to come up with solutions.

In addition to the fulfilment I felt from assisting others, I also had a successful business and a good paycheck. I became satisfied with my job to the point where I stopped putting my singing career first. My work attracted a sizable following, and hundreds of people looked to me for advice and considered me to be their mentor.

I experienced a sense of serenity and true happiness, and the glow that had long since vanished from my face was back. My life changed for the better as a result of the influence of philosophy and spirituality. I read books, including religious materials, and the information I discovered during this time had a big influence. This year was a turning point that fundamentally altered my outlook on life. I no longer felt fear because I now had a profound grasp of what it meant to be human. I came to the knowledge that I was just a human being, nothing more, nothing less, and that feeling of serenity and satisfaction came with that.

13.

PEOPLE ARE WEIRD

With so many people around me, I even tried playing online games and found that I was very good at them. Because everything seemed to be going smoothly, I had the impression that I was in a dream. I had no partner, yet I was genuinely happy. I had a lot of requests from female friends and admirers who looked up to me as a mentor. I made the decision not to take any of them, though, as I had eventually discovered happiness and fulfilment in my own company.

While I was spending time with one of my favourite people in December, I unexpectedly got a text from Naina. This surprised me, so I started talking to her about it. Although it turned out to be a constructive discussion, she brought up an odd topic that was connected to my background. She made a strange comment that piqued my interest.

Naina was an unexpected turn of events. She disclosed that she was aware of my recovery from my diaphragm problem. She expressed her regrets to me before blocking me. I was perplexed by her unexpected actions and wished I knew more about what she meant by her comment. I became completely perplexed in the days that followed as a result of Naina's texts. I made the choice to call her and discuss the problem to get clarification. She agreed to meet with me in person but refused to speak with me to answer my queries.

When I finally met her at the conference, it seemed like it had just been yesterday that we had gone through our separation. However, I was able to manage my emotions this time. Naina gave me a quick hug before apologising. I initially thought her apology was for our previous breakup, but I soon understood it was something completely different this time. She said something that profoundly disturbed me psychologically and disturbed my sense of calm.

She was the one who taught me about spirituality because she independently learned about it and conducted research on it. She learned about my issues with my physical and mental health after she got married and wanted to support me. I got upset with her since I had entrusted her with so much and shared practically everything with her. However, when she claimed she still loved me, I broke down in tears since I too truly loved her. But somehow I controlled my emotions and walked away from her without saying good-bye. My eyes began to well up with tears as I realised how deeply I loved her, but I never told her.

For the whole day, My mind was filled with thoughts of the time I had spent with her as I lay on my bed at home. Knowing that I had made the appropriate choice about who to love at that precise moment gave me a deep sense of joy. She loved me in an unfathomably special way, and our love was unadulterated.

It was now time for me to get back to work. I went to the doctor for routine checkups to make sure I was healthy. In addition, I obtained my first digital certificate as an entrepreneur after spending five months putting in significant study time. This success served as proof of the work I put into starting my own business. My diaphragm muscle's recuperation is the only part of my journey that is still to be completed, and I am holding out hope that it will do so quickly.

But I got betrayed by her because she had been tracking me for the last three years, and I told her everything without knowing the truth. I was blaming myself again and again that, after a long time, I trusted someone, and that person completely used and betrayed me. I knew that her intentions were pure and harmless, but still, it was another heartbreaking moment for me. Now, every day, Nains started visiting in my dreams, and I couldn't get sleep because of her. As time passed, my sleeping issues got more serious, and once again, I found myself exhausted. Even after a few days, I noticed I had some hallucinations of her, and it started bothering me very much.

To distract myself from these things, I wanted to start my own shoe business. I went to Delhi and looked for the shoe market. I spent some time there, and because I was travelling, I wanted to get some sleep. So I was looking for a room where I could get some rest. A random guy came to me and told me about the room in his guest house. For me, it was a good deal for a worthy amount. I started following him, and we reached there. As I entered the room, a lady came to me and asked me for the rent. I gave her rent, and within a few minutes, that guy came with another guy. They both had a knife, and they took my money and my mobile phone. By seeing this, I got nervous and fainted there, and now all of them are scared. They tried to wake me up, and after a few attempts, I opened my eyes. I took my time, and that lady gave me tea and water. After having tea, I was fully aware, and that guy returned my mobile and a few rupees so I could get back home. I didn't notify my family about this, but I shared my experience with my close friends. I came back home, but for the next few days, I wasn't able to sleep because that incident was haunting me in my dream. I started my meditation and other spiritual activities again so I could recover myself from these things.

Two years ago, I met a random girl named Gauri while I was offering consulting services through my social media handles. We instantly bonded and grew close. She appeared innocent and a little naive. She used to talk to me about everything that concerned her, and she always saw me as a mentor. Likewise, I thought highly of her as a person. As the years went by, we became closer and eventually even revealed our secrets to one another.

More so than our family, we trusted one another. She was the one who stood by me the most, even during my most trying times. I suppose it was because I had a lot of respect for her. She was always there for me, no matter how difficult the circumstances were. We frequently sang in unison since she was also a singer. Additionally, we could jam well together.

She had a really toxic partner who never let her act freely. I didn't like him, but I never told her that. Gauri frequently confided in me about her problems with her lover, but I never gave her my honest opinion out of fear of hurting her feelings. I'm not sure why, but seeing her upset always made me angry.

She was the only one I kept in touch with while I withdrew from society and withdrew within myself to heal. We grew closer to one another as time went on. She contacted me one day and broke the unexpected news that her partner had dumped her for another woman. I had never seen her cry before, so simply hearing her voice when she was doing it broke me. At that point, all I wanted was to be with her. She seemed to have significance for me. I didn't feel a romantic connection to her, but I did care for her a lot.

We didn't talk much, but I could tell she was feeling something. She wasn't the only one crying that day; I was crying for her as well. It was very hard for me to keep my emotions in check after seeing her like this because she was the one who had shielded me from many things.

After a few days, I was pleased to discover that she had finally recovered from the breakup. She behaved a little more sternly and quietly this time, which made it unpleasant for me because we never acted like this when we met. I never made her act in a typical manner. I always attempted to calm her down whenever she became emotional, since I knew what it was like to live with heartbreak. My goal was to be there for her and assist her as she went through the recovery process.

She had a middle-aged bachelor cousin who was single. She had previously been betrayed by him, and I recall her coming to me to ask for an apology on behalf of her cousin. I initially turned down her offer because I thought someone who had misled her before might do it again. She suggested that we give him a chance, though.

That person always seemed to be aware of her and wanted her to tell him everything in detail so he could give her advice. They hadn't spoken in a while, so how did he manage to learn so much about her breakup? This one thing looked very strange to me.

Gauri provided me with screenshots of their communication since I always double-checked the advice he gave Gauri as a consultant. He was completely unaware of my presence, by the way.

I was a little taken aback by what I saw him telling her because it appeared to me that he was flattering her in an effort to win her over. However, I never told Gauri about this finding since I wanted her to make up her own mind about everything. I thought she should make her own decisions about the problem without my input.

Gauri was about 22 years old, and that guy was 37 years old. He was getting creepier and creepier as time went on. I've always been curious about what kind of intentions he had for her based on how he texted her. For the first time, I warned Gauri, but she responded that she shouldn't be concerned because this was just how he always behaved and interacted with others.

I once required a bank employee's assistance with some task and didn't have any connections there. Gauri and I had this conversation, and she promised to speak with her cousin. I spoke to him and got to know him for the first time since that individual had connections there. I met him at the bank, and the vibes I was getting from him were a little bit abnormal. He was a person with a dual-faced personality because he was just giving me so much attention while I was just behaving normally. I sensed very negative vibes from him, and I told everything to Gauri and warned her about her cousin. Unfortunately, she misinterpreted my worry and believed that I just wanted her to spend time with me because I was insecure around other people.

It was important for me to make it clear that I wasn't feeling uncomfortable out of any sort of jealousy or insecurity, but rather because of the strange signals I was getting from him. It was the first time she questioned me, and while at first I didn't mind it, I started to worry a little about her. Now Gauri behaves differently, and it appears that she is constantly attempting to conceal something from me. I'm worried about the shift in her conduct since I appreciate our friendship and want her to feel at ease enough to be open and honest with me.

After a few days, I unexpectedly received a call from my ex. We had a brief discussion. Gauri informed me later that evening that she was aware of my ex's call. I was surprised and questioned how she discovered it. She acknowledged that she had been in touch with my ex and had discussed practically everything about me with her after I had continually questioned her. I had no idea why she would divulge such personal information to my ex, so when I heard this, I was utterly horrified. I was uncomfortable and confused about our friendship after this revelation. I came to the realisation that I needed to have a serious discussion with Gauri in order to ascertain her goals and establish some ground rules for confidentiality and trust.

She lied to me and revealed my information without my permission, so I stopped talking to her for a few days. Now, I've had several inquiries from random Instagram accounts. It appears that someone is keeping an eye on me and trying to keep tabs on everything I do. For a few days, I turned off all of my social media accounts. One day, Gauri called and asked to talk about something. But I wasn't in the mood, so I didn't really chat with her. I already had a small amount of resentment toward her, so I requested that she not call for a bit. Because of how I was acting, she became irate and contacted me again later that night. We had the worst conversation because I lost my tolerance this time.

For the first time ever, we went a week without speaking to one another, and we didn't even want to. I never told her how much I missed her, though. My birthday was the following week, and she failed to wish me I hadn't anticipated this from her, so I became overly upset.

I blocked her phone number and deleted her from my social media accounts after that day. I was crying as I did this because I would do anything to keep her. Although I was angry with her, my spirit still yearned for her. I was aware that everything for us was about to end. Though it was a challenging choice, I believed it was essential for my emotional wellbeing.

After a few days, I learned through a local person that a middle-aged man was requesting my details. I wasn't sure who this could be, but then I wondered if maybe it was her cousin seeking me out. But because he already had my number, it was rather scary and uncomfortable that he didn't just call. The fact that he went to a total stranger to ask about me instead created more questions about his motivations. I became anxious and unsure of the entire situation as a result.

When I called him to find out why he was hunting for me, he threatened me without cause. I spoke to him respectfully at first, but after he responded to my questions inanely, I yelled at him. Threats abounded throughout the debate.

After a few days, the police station called me to let me know that someone had filed a police report accusing me of threatening them. I went there to deal with the situation since I was positive that it was that individual. He arrived fully prepared with his version of events, which surprised me.

I was questioned extensively by the police officer, and I gave honest responses to all of them. They did want me to apologise in writing for my behaviour, though. The worst day of my life was when they punished me by sending me to a room. My father and brother arrived at the station after the police called my family. As a part of the grievance-resolution procedure, I sent the complainant a letter of apology.

In the evening, I returned home while still reeling from the experience. I couldn't force myself to eat anything that day since my father was so angry with me, and I went to bed that night feeling emotionally spent. I had a lot of unanswered questions because I had no idea what was going on in my life. I went to the police station after first losing my best friend. I finally went through a long period of tension and insomnia.

I had a terrible headache after a few days. It was somewhat painful at first, but after four or five days, the agony increased. I tried using medications to help, but they weren't as helpful this time. I visited the doctor for a checkup, and after doing certain tests, he identified the issue as a migraine. I questioned why it occurred to me, and he responded that it was because of excessive stress. I started using medication to get some relief, although occasionally I struggled with thinking control. Therefore, the drugs weren't very effective. I attempted to meditate to reduce my stress, but this time I was unable to do so due to an overthinking loop.

I made numerous attempts to get in touch with Gauri but never received a response. I merely wanted to dispel all of the uncertainties that existed at the moment. I couldn't sleep, and occasionally, I didn't get any rest for three to four weeks. My mental health was severely impacted by that event. Since I don't get enough sleep, I experience nighttime hallucinations. I could make out a few strange shadows, which terrifies me greatly. Additionally, I've discovered that occasionally my body doesn't function properly; it looks as though various sections of my body briefly get immobilised.

It is now a significant issue for me. I visited the doctor and informed him of all that had been going on. It was hemiplegic migraine symptoms, he claimed. My body could become permanently paralyzed if this problem worsens because it is also incurable.

I started taking the right medication and temporarily isolated myself. I restarted my spiritual activities after receiving some relief from the drugs because I really wanted to get rid of my migraine problem as soon as possible. To recover from this issue, I had to put in over 4 months of demanding training. My opinion of individuals has been greatly impacted by all of these encounters. I was betrayed by several people at once, so I now find it difficult to put my trust in anyone.

Why do I call myself a UNCULTURED ARTIST

Since I was repeatedly betrayed by my own people, I've practically finished everything. Although I almost moved on from that incident, I still occasionally feel the effects of all these things. I used to be one of the healthiest people before music, which always surprises me. Now I realise that I occasionally experience things like food poisoning, migraines, and other medical conditions. I always tried to avoid medications, but sometimes circumstances were beyond my control.

I now had certain questions in my head that I would like to have answered. I was aware of someone who could provide answers to these questions. I had made the decision to see her one last time. We had a brief phone talk after I gave her a call. I asked her to meet with me during the call, and she accepted.

We had broken up more than six years prior, but we still had some sort of feelings for each other. She admitted that she was shocked that I had called to arrange our meeting before our meal at the restaurant.

I had so many things to discuss and wanted to revisit every single moment that happened in the past.

Me- It had been a long time, but still, it seems like we are looking and feeling like we used to for each other before.

She - No, it's not like that. I don't feel anything for you, and I think you are still there waiting for me.

Me - Well, after all of these shitstorms, I have no respect for you.

She- Then why do you want to see me?

Me - Well, you left me when I was going through the worst of my life, and you came back to help me. Why?

She - I just wanted to help you.

Me - At that point, you still love me, right?

And if you loved me at that time, then why didn't you come back even though you knew that I was still in love with you?

Me - You talked to me on a regular basis, and you knew this, but still. Even whenever I tried to approach someone, it was you who stopped me every time.

She - I stopped you because I didn't want to suffer again. I cared for you.

Me - I was suffering because of you, and I was just pretending that I didn't need anyone, but in reality, I actually need someone who takes care of me. I deserve someone too, but you always tried to keep me away from this. Why did you do that?

She - It's not true; I was always there for you whenever you needed me. And I never tried to keep you away from anyone.

Me- Is it? You didn't have the guts to reveal your real character, and you are saying that you were there for me.

Me - I would have been committed to that girl to whom I was going to propose, even though she had feelings for me, because of you, I left her.

She - Well, if you ask me, it wasn't me; it was you who stopped himself. If you were sure about that person, why have you always come to me? You wanted someone who could provide everything you wanted; that's why you are insecure about everyone, and this is the reason you are still looking for someone, and believe me, you will not get anyone if you want your expectations to be fulfilled.

She - Did I ask you about my partner when I left you?

Did I ever share anything about my marriage? You know why, because I know every single person has their own good or bad things.

She - But you always want perfection in everything; that's why you are still paying for your own actions.

Me - So, according to you, it was my fault. I'm just protecting my emotions.

She - You know one thing: I knew that you were going to suffer from all of those things because of your own methods.

Me - So you knew that, and instead of helping me, you just left me.

She- You had slapped me when I tried to stop you. Now you are saying that I wasn't there.

She - You even left everyone because you never wanted to listen to someone's advice.

Me - But no one was able to understand what I was going through. I just wanted someone who could listen to me.

She - You already had that person as a friend, but what did you do to her? You played with her emotions so you could get distracted from your own problems.

Me - How do you know that? What I did to her.

She - It was me who sent her to you because she genuinely loved you. After my marriage, She came to me and shared everything with me, so I shared your condition, but still, she accepted you even at your worst.

She - But you played with her feelings not by using her, but by showing fake love.

Me - I didn't love her, but I tried to love her, but when I realized that I had no feelings for her, I just told her everything and left her.

She - It's not you who left her; it was her who left you. Even though you tried to contact her, you got no response from her side. You know you betrayed her.

She - And then I realised it was difficult for you to recover, so I changed my identity and came to you because I knew that it was only me who could support you at that moment.

She - Stop blaming me for your own actions.

Me - Well, I am not blaming you or myself either. But I can sense what is going to happen in the future.

Me - This is the reason I don't trust people easily. I can read their minds and listen to their unspoken words.

She - So you think you can sense the future? Do I look like a fool to you?

She - Now that you are doing things like problem-solving and providing consulting, you are just doing this because you don't want to get bothered by your past.

She - You have to accept this and move on, because one day even I will not be there for you.

Me - Well, I am not blaming you or myself either. But I can see and sense the future through vibes.

She - So you think you can sense the future? Do I look like a fool to you?

Me - Trust me, I can see your future too. and the most disturbing thing I can see is that I can't see anything for you.

Me - One day I will talk to someone about you, and at that time you will be just a memory and nothing.

She - You are just spreading your hate. I am leaving now. Please take care of yourself. Good bye

The moment she left, I could see her future, and I knew that her life would end in the near future. After this, she finally left, and I was there, thinking about each and every day of my life, and there was an unexplained silence on my face. I came back home and sat in front of the mirror. I was looking at myself, and there were hundreds of questions in my mind.

14.

MYCKIEE - PHILOSOPHICAL MONK

Yes, I become a little bit insecure about people, but that doesn't mean I am running away from something; I am just trying to explore more people as much as I can, and I want to help people through some philosophy. Now I am at that stage of my life where I become different from the inside. Since my childhood, I have always preferred sentiments over other things, but now I can see different perspectives in one situation. I can sense other people's emotions. I can see their thoughts and read their faces. I can feel the universe with my eyes closed. I am still emotional, but at the same time, I can control it whenever I want to. People around me feel comfortable somehow; it doesn't matter what age group they are in.

Today, I see the whole world from different perspectives, and even my ethics have become more practical. Even at the religious level, I have become more disciplined. I know who the superior power is and what he wants from us. I can sense him; he is inside me. The people who I used to know in the past are now strangers to me, and I am completely fine with this. In the past, I went through multiple betrayals and failures, but I still have no hatred for anyone. Yes, I am still upset with them, but I don't want to hurt them at any cost. In other words, I want nothing from them. They are human beings like me, and humans do make mistakes. Even I had made mistakes too.

I still teach people about spirituality and philosophy and always try to enlighten them. It actually makes me happy. It's like my job for the whole world. I don't know, but I feel this world needs a whole new perspective. I feel that without spirituality and philosophical knowledge, we can't achieve the true potential of human beings. Things like education, the internet, and entertainment stuff are limitations for us. We have to enlighten ourselves; only then will we know about ourselves.

Well, our lives all depend on our karma. People think that karma is all about our actions, but this is not true. Our actions and thinking both play an important role. Our mind is like a magnet; it will attract whatever you want to attract, but most people think about those things, which have nothing to do with reality. That's why they face so many problems and instability in their lives. Well, I wasn't aware of this either, but now I understand how my thoughts affect my life, and I try to avoid every negative and baseless thought.

Well, being a musician, I always thought that music was the best gift to us by nature, but at the same time, I felt something strange about some tracks, like sometimes it actually makes me depressed. Even in my childhood, it did the same thing to me. So I was always curious to know why this thing always happened to me.

But as time passed, I learned about meditation, psychology, and philosophy. I understand a little bit of this theory. For me, music actually affects our aura and mind. Music is a simple combination of some frequencies, and these frequencies act differently from person to person. So people have no idea what they are listening to; they simply enjoy that particular beat, harmony, and vocals, but they don't know what they are attracted to. Sad songs are the best example. It's just a mixture of some sad lyrics with negative harmony, and people can relate to it.

Our brains can't differentiate between good and bad things. It only wants a moment of joy; it doesn't matter where it is coming from.

Well, if lyrical music is full of positive thoughts, then it is good, but if someone wrote some lyrics because he was feeling depressed and just expressed his feelings through those lyrics, then it would affect their listeners too. When I was exploring the darkest areas of the world, I got to know that elite people never listen to these things; they have their own music, so they can't get distracted.

There are many artists around us who are doing the same stuff again and again because they know that most of their audience is emotionally weak, and they are doing their business by manipulating their audience sentiments. I belonged to Punjab, and the music here is completely shit. I never understood what they were talking about. There are artists who are just brainwashing their audience with their nonsensical tracks. I mean, common man, our lives are not about alcohol, doing violence, dating and banging girls, or satisfying our egos. I always wondered who funded them because it couldn't be done by a group of people. I am pretty sure the government, the Mafia, and the elite people are playing a major role in this.

The same thing goes for Hindi and other music industries. They only have two topics, one on romance and the other on clubbing. This is not true; life is not about these things. We are all here for the betterment of society, but we are getting this.

Ashiqui is the most pathetic thing these movies taught us. They have already brainwashed almost 3–4 generations because they always want to earn money; they don't give a shit about our mentality. Still, we have no idea what the actual meaning of love is. These movies created a false dynamic with the name Ashiqui. 3 Idiots was the movie that actually had huge hype in those days. When I watched that movie, I was shocked to see what was happening. The main character had dated the principal daughter because he was a little bit overconfident with his bullshit theories. Even that character almost humiliated that girl's father as a whole. After that movie, the whole generation started engineering, and today, 70% of them are unemployed.

I am not saying Hollywood movies are the best; they are a complete waste of your time. Just watch good movies, which will add some good perspective to your life.

The same thing goes for the movie industry, except for a few movies. The same thing is happening again and again, even now that they are introducing soft porn culture, and the most shocking part is that the government is supporting this. Well, government is nothing; they are just a bunch of people who just want to rule their city, state, and country, not for the other people but for their own benefits.Even in my study, all I can say is that government is the reason behind everything. They just manipulate people, and people follow and trust their words.

We see the world through our eyes, and we see the people around us and what they are doing. The same thing goes for the movies. I am not saying to stop watching movies or TV serials, but we should ask ourselves why we are watching them. See, Hindi cinema has already brainwashed our whole generation. Still, people are suffering from one-sided love. Still, people believe in this theory that life is incomplete without romantic love. Spend your time with yourself, I don't think there is anything in this world that can be more beautiful than this.

I see people just spending most of their time on the mobile, and they are living in the virtual world more than the real world, and when the day ends, they find themselves more depressed. We are living in an era where social media influencers earn more than PhD holders, even more than CAs. This one thing tells us that our society is going in the completely wrong direction, and this one thing is completely beneficial for us because if we see our competitors already trapped in this thing.

People admire these influencers. I mean common man. If someone is not telling you about human psychology, money psychology, our moral values, etc., if they are just entertaining you through their content, believe me, they are not worth your time. Remove these people from your life. They are just building their lives and fortunes. The worst thing is that you will not meet these people in real life, so ask yourself, Why are we watching them?

Even they know one thing: their content is making their audience insecure but still they don't care. The bad thing about today's generation is that they have no time for themselves. Well, one more thing: because of this social media, people face depression and anxiety, and to get rid of this, they use other social media platforms. It's like an infinity loop, and few know about it.

Boys are slowly becoming girls, and girls are becoming more masculine, and because of this change, the chances of a breakup in a relationship and divorce rates are getting worse. Females are the ones who value emotions, and men symbolise strength, but today's scenario is getting different. I have noticed that many boys need emotional support more than girls. The reason is that when they use these platforms, and the influencers out there are out of their league, their body standards almost define perfection.

When a guy who is not so physically fit, doesn't have access to things, or doesn't have a rich background or educated family feels insecure, they feel insecure because girls around them are already seeing the best product out there, and these guys are nowhere close to them. So this one particular thing is killing the most youth, and the same thing goes for the girl too. I saw many girl influencers who showed and used their bodies to attract a young audience.

People are still trying their best to impress others; we can't impress everyone with our skills; some people will like it, some will not. Rejections are the most common thing in our lives. I can even say people get rejected in everything because we have some expectations, and when the output we get is not as expected, we get hurt. So we should understand this: we will get rejections for every possible thing we have in our lives.

Well, if we talk about ourselves, I mean humans, I can say we are the best and worst creations of nature. We can understand, we can learn, and we can feel we can do anything, but still, people are doing weird things for their survival. There is no actual bond between any human, not even in family. Family is just a man-made term where people are playing a role that is given to them by society. By the way, I am in support of this because if we remove our family, we will have nothing. We make friends on the basis of our own comfort zone, with the person to whom we can relate ourselves, and so many other things, but sometimes we get betrayed by these people.

Even the only thing I got from humans was betrayal, so I am too concerned about this thing. Why people betray each other—this one thing always makes me think deeply about human psychology. See, when a person who made their own mind and decision for their own benefits betrays others through this process, he or she actually takes the true core value from that person, and the person on the other's side is like a skeleton to them. That person will question himself or herself, doubt himself or herself for those questions where he or she has no one to answer, and that person will also be stuck in a loop of overthinking. Even if you ask me, it's almost like hell. So if someone betrays you once, please don't ever trust that person again because they already made you believe that humans are weird and selfish.

I do trust people, like 1 out of 100 (from my known ones), and people around me know that I don't trust them, even though I always said don't trust me either. Because my own ethics and ideology may crush their soul, if you know nothing about me, please don't trust me and don't expect anything from me. I will disappoint you in some aspects.

I still remember when Naina left me; those were the days when I was in a room full of darkness. It took some years for me to recover, and there are plenty of things I have learned from that incident. Love doesn't exist in real life; it is just an image of that person to which we are attracted and attached. When we generate or create another perception of that person, we have some other feelings for that person. So things like love and hate don't exist. We are the ones who actually implant the idea of liking and wanting someone with whom we can spend our time so we can get some happy moments.

Attachment is a term that we can consider to mean bonding with someone, having a relationship, and putting in heavy emotional effort for someone. Whenever we don't get that kind of result in return, we get hurt and start hurting ourselves because all of our efforts mean nothing to that person. This one thing starts killing us from inside because now that individual's one action decides how we will respond.

Just ask yourself: Why do we need that person? It might give you some good moments, but it will be temporary for us. I am not saying don't get married or don't get in relationships; I am just saying value your emotions above everything. Protect them at every cost. There are 8 billion people around us. Everyone is different in their own way, so we can't give our full emotions to one or two people. If we spend our time and give all of our emotions to one person, then we will die mentally in the future, for sure. People will leave us one day. I mean, each and every individual will leave us. We will leave this planet one day. So when we are living our lives, we should spend that time on ourselves. Be a great human being, both spiritually and through your philosophy. Earn as much money as you can so you can experience and explore the world more. The more you explore the world, the more you understand humans.

Well, I have my own philosophy where I see the world a little bit differently, and because of my past incidents, I have become a little weird because I see things from various perspectives. A few days ago, I got to know that Naina passed away in an accident. I was shocked a little bit, but I already knew this; it didn't affect me much. Finally, now I can approach someone for the rest of my life. Well, I always tried to control my emotions and had always played in defensive mode, but this one particular thing made me weaker.

My father hasn't talked to me in a normal way for the last 8 years, and I have lost almost all of my finances. Even my close ones have now become strangers to me, but I am fine with everything. One thing that hurts me the most is that when I was in depression and fighting against all of my problems, no one came for help (except a few). Even at my worst, I always try to help others, but one thing I sensed from those people too was that they only needed my help; they didn't need me, and once my job was done, they became strangers too. Well, I have so many people in my life, and most of them admire me, but because of past incidents, somehow my perception for people has changed now. I do trust people, but I only say these words so the other person can feel comfortable, but in reality, I don't trust anyone (except two). Well, I don't want to trust anyone anymore, at any cost. Still, I pretend and show other people that I trust them, but I can't trust anyone. Because of spirituality, I can sense anything, like if I am talking to someone, even by texting or calling, I can sense their intentions or what is going on in their mind. And 90% of the time, people are faking their emotions, and I know this, but I never show anything to them. This is one of the reasons that I don't want to trust anyone.

Now my diaphragm problem has completely recovered. I healed my migraine with reiki energy and healing techniques, and after a long time, I am completely healthy. There are many things I want to achieve now, and I was waiting for this moment. I want to share my story so people around me can understand the reason behind my ideology and philosophy, because I may disappoint them in the future and I want them to expect nothing from my side.

Someone will like me, and someone will hate me.

Someone will call me the strongest one, and someone will call me a crying baby.

Someone will appreciate my ethics, and someone will criticise them.

Someone will call me the one who follows God's words, and someone will call me the devil.

Someone will call me an artistic genius, and someone will call me highly self-obsessed.

Someone will call me a gem, and someone will call me an egoistic bastard.

Someone will follow my guidance, and someone will counter them.

Well, I can't blame any of them because it all depends on how they approach me, what kind of priorities they have, and how they make their perception towards something, and I always said, 'I SEEM TO BE WHAT I AM NOT YOU SEE'

To be continued.....